COOKING WITH KATERINA

Traditional Cretan Recipes

Copyright 2015 – Katerina Goniotaki

All rights reserved. No part of this publication may be reproduced, stored in a retrieval system or transmitted by any means or form, electronically, mechanically, by photocopy audio recording or otherwise without the prior permission of the author, in accordance with Copyright Law.

Black Bay Publishing

TITLE - Cooking With Katerina
AUTHOR – Katerina Goniotaki
COPYRIGHT – Katerina Goniotaki
www.blackbaypublishing.com
LAYOUT – Black Bay Publishing

Please feel free to contact Katerina if you want more information about staying at her apartments in Tavronitis.

Why not follow Haridimos Apartments on Facebook and be kept up to date with all our current events and special offers.

www.facebook.com/pages/Haridimos-Apartments

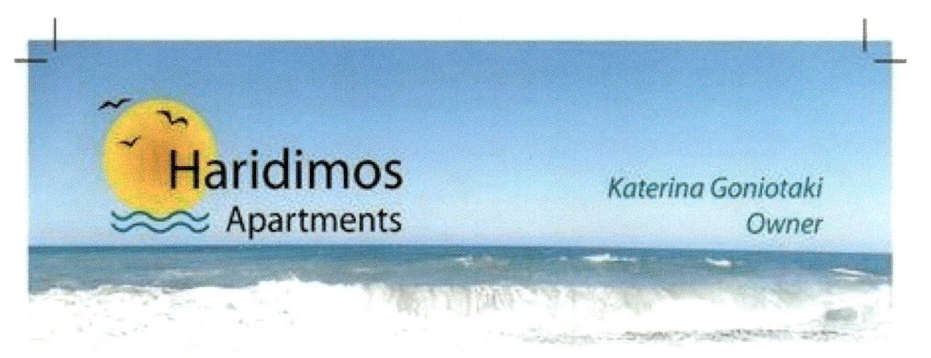

Haridimos Apartments

Katerina Goniotaki
Owner

Self catering accommodation Tavronitis, Chania, Creta, TK 73006
0030 28240 23638 hotel/fax   e-mail: haridimosapts@yahoo.gr
0030 28210 62170 home/fax   skype name: katarinahardimos
0030 69369 07363 Katerina's mobile   www.haridimos-apartments.gr

For details on how to get your book published please go to
www.BlackBayPublishing.com

E-mail the publishing assistant, Andrew Morgan at
Andrew.Blackbaypublishing@gmail.com

For general enquiries contact us at
Blackbaypublishing@gmail.com

Cooking With Katerina

CONTENTS

ONE – THE CRETAN DIET	11
TWO – OLIVE OIL	12
THREE – ABOUT THE AUTHOR	14
FOUR –TRADITIONAL DIPS	**16**
TZATZIKI	16
MELITZANOSALATA – Aubergine Dip	18
SKORDALIA – Garlic Dip	20
HOUMOUS or *HUMMUS*– Chick-pea Puree	23
FAVA – Split-Pea Dip	25
KOKKINOYOULIA YIA SALATA – Beetroot Salad	27
FIVE – STARTERS & APPETIZERS	**30**

GIGANTES – Butter Beans	30
KOLOKITHOKEFTEDES - Fried Zucchini Balls	33
MARATHO PITES – Fennel Pies	36
SFAKIAN PIE – Cheese Pie with honey	39
SAGANAKI TYRI – Fried Cheese	42
PATATES KEFTEDES – Fried Potato Balls	44
DOLMADAKIA – Stuffed Vine Leaves	46
FASOLADA – Bean Soup	49
ALMYRO ZAMBON KAI TYRI TOURTA – Salty ham and cheese cake	51

SIX – MAIN COURSES　　　　　　　　　　　　53

BOUREKI	53
MOUSSAKA	57
YEMISTA – Stuffed Peppers and Tomato	61
SOUTSOUKAKIA – Spiced Meat Balls	64
BRIAM – Traditional Vegetarian Dish	68
STIFADO – Beef or Rabbit in red wine sauce	70
KLEFTIKO – *Hidden Meat* Pie	73
BAKALAOS – Cod with Garlic	77
IMAM BALDI – Stuffed Aubergines	80
SOUPIA – Cuttlefish in Red Wine Sauce	84
PASTITSIO	86

SEVEN – DESSERTS　　　　　　　　　　　　　90

LOUKOUMADES – Fried Honey Balls	90
GALAKTOBOUREKO – Custard Pie	94
KALITSOUNIA – Cheese Pies (With Honey)	97
BAKLAVA – Sweet flaky pastry with nuts	102
KRASOKOULORA – Cookies made with wine	105
SFOUNGARI LEMONI - Lemon Sponge	107
ROSAKIA – Mini Chocolate Swirl Cakes	111

Katerina Goniotaki was born on the beautiful island of Crete and has been cooking for as long as she could reach the stove top.

Using recipes and traditions handed down through her family from generation to generation, Katerina will guide you through the delights of traditional Cretan cooking using only the freshest ingredients and helping you to enjoy the healthy Mediterranean Diet.

With full colour pictures and step-by-step instructions, **'Cooking With Katerina'** will have you preparing the finest Cretan cuisine for your family in no time.

HARIDIMOS APARTMENTS
TAVRONITIS, CRETE
www.haridimos-apartments.gr

Introduction

Crete, the largest of the Greek Islands and the fifth largest of the Mediterranean is an island full of traditions and charm that delights the visitor.

From the terraced hills, laden with their famous olive trees, to the beautiful shorelines and the local fisherman displaying his day's catch, wherever you go in Crete you will find a glimpse of the wonderful food that nature provides.

The local people are proud of their history and culture, and rightfully so. Nowhere else in the Mediterranean has faced more invasions and been more terribly treated as the Cretans. Their strategically placed island connects the West to the East and Europe to Africa and has been classed a rich prize since man first learnt to sail.

You would think this history of aggression and occupation would have made the Cretan people distant and wary of strangers, but nothing could be further from the truth. The rule of *filoxenia*, or kindness to strangers, is still an important and practiced tradition. Walkers will find themselves offered lifts from farmers in pick-up trucks or a couple out doing their daily trip to the bakery. It is often a case that you will be offered a glass of water or an orange as you stroll around a village in the mid-day sun as a welcome gift to quench your thirst.

The Cretan people truly are some of the friendliest and genuine personalities that you can meet and none more so than Katerina, her husband Hari and their wonderful family, who run the Haridimos apartments in Tavronitis.

Enjoy your stay in Crete, and as I am sure you will hear many times during your visit to this beautiful island…

Yiamas.

Ian Yates - 2015

Cooking With Katerina

One – The Cretan Diet

In research conducted by the Rockefeller Institute, the Cretan diet is based mainly around *'foodstuff of vegetatitive origin: cereals, vegetables, fruit and olive oil.'*

It is this diet that makes the Cretan people some of the healthiest in the world with less heart disease per capita than many other countries, including Japan. The significant findings showed that the Crete diet takes almost 40% of its calorific intake from Olive Oil which is rich in vitamins, monounsaturates and essential antioxidants that protect the heart from disease and has been shown to help reduce the growth of certain cancers. The importance of Olive Oil in the preparation and as a dressing on many of the day-to-day foods that are eaten by Cretans plays a significant part in their healthy make-up.

Seafood has an important place in the diet but historic overfishing of the Mediterranean has reduced the amount of fish served in many homes. Chicken, lamb, goat, pork and rabbit are the meats of choice, and many people in the outlying towns and villages of Crete will have a small area where they keep their animals, even if it is just a few chickens kept for their eggs and meat.

All of the dishes in this book are made using the freshest ingredients, some picked straight from Katerina's garden in the seconds before use. Don't worry if you have to use supermarket bought items for the recipes, the dishes will still taste marvellous and be healthy in the way that only the Cretan Diet can be.

Kali Orexi – Bon Appetite – Enjoy Your Meal

Two – Olive Oil

Olive Oil is regarded as one of the so called super-foods that can aid the immune system to prevent diseases, assist in the formation of healthy skin and bones and can be used in the treatment and prevention of diabetes to name just a few of its remarkable properties. The fact that Olive Oil also tastes fantastic whether used as a dressing, a dip for bread or when used in cooking is an added bonus.

Olive Oil has been used for thousands of years as a food in Crete and the olive trees can be seen covering the hills and valleys with their lush, green, year round vegetation. The trees and the oil they produced are still revered by the Cretan people because they can offer so much to a family. An olive grove can provide economic stability for families with oil and firewood being an important source of income away from the summer months.

Crete also consumes more olive oil per head than any other nation. A study in 1996 showed the Cretans consume 31 litres per person each year; the world average in comparison is 18 litres per person. With figures like these it is easy to see why olive oil is such an important part in the daily lifestyle of Crete and its people.

There are three basic 'grades' of Olive Oil;

i. Extra Virgin Olive Oil – Made from the first cold-pressing and with no chemicals or hot water methods of extraction allowed. It must have an acidity of less than one per cent and is the best of all the olive oils.

ii. Virgin Olive Oil – Also made from the first cold-pressing of the olives, but the acidity levels can be higher; normally between 1% and 3%.

iii. Pure Olive Oil – Flavour can vary, but acidity is the same as for Virgin Olive Oil. It is produced from a blend of Olive Oils, and whilst 100% pure it is not best suited for use in dressings, but should be used in cooking where it imparts the flavours of the oil without burning at high temperatures.

12 Benefits of Olive Oil

Type II Diabetes – Olive oil diet is rich in monosaturated fats which helps protect against Type II diabetes.

Obesity – Olive oil can make it easier to control or lose weight due to its high nutrient value.

Heart Health – Helps slow down heart aging process, antioxidants may offer protection against red blood cells damage.

Blood Pressure – Taking olive oil on a daily basis can help reduce hypertension.

Keeps Bones Healthy – Help prevent the loss of calcium related to developing osteoporosis during later years.

Relieving Earache – Olive oil is known as being a natural remedy for earache and for dealing with excess ear wax.

Depression – People who follow a Mediterranean style diet that is rich in olive oil may be at a lower risk of depression.

Damaged Hair – Olive oil has the ability to moisturize hair that has become frizzy or dry.

Colon Cancer – Research by Spanish scientists has shown including olive oil in the diet lowers the risk of this cancer.

Skin Health – It's used in skincare products as it's full of antioxidants and vitamins A and E.

Skin Cancer – Olive oil is rich in antioxidants, and may help lower the risk of malignant melanomas.

Digestion – Helps to give a feeling of fullness, and the contents of the stomach are digested more slowly.

www.HomeTipsWorld.com

Sources:
http://www.oliveoiltimes.com/olive-oil-health-benefits
http://www.thedailygreen.com/green-homes/latest/olive-oil-benefits-uses-460609
http://www.sciencedaily.com/releases/2009/04/090401200447.htm
http://www.healingdaily.com/detoxification-diet/olive-oil.htm
http://www.internationaloliveoil.org/estaticos/view/91-olive-oil-and-blood-pressure

Three – About the Author

Katerina Goniotaki was born near the city of Chania on the Greek island of Crete. With her husband, Hari, and their family, they run the Haridimos Apartments in the coastal village of Tavronitis in North-West Crete.

She has been cooking with her mother, also called Katerina, since she was a small child and they still use the recipes that have been handed down through the generations from mother to daughter.

All of the dishes in this book are used in her restaurant at the Haridimos Apartments and are lovingly prepared using only the freshest ingredients.

Katerina and Hari welcome you to the delights of Cretan cooking and if you are ever in Tavronitis please pop in and say hello. You will always be assured of a very warm welcome…

                        YIAMAS

COOKING WITH KATERINA AND MAMA

Why not learn to cook traditional Cretan food with your host at the Haridimos Apartments?

Using only the freshest ingredients you will learn all about the healthy Cretan Diet, how to prepare some magnificent dishes, and best of all, you get to eat the food you make afterwards!

Greek cuisine

From hearty stews, to warming soups and simple side dishes, traditional Greek food combines the freshest of ingredients from land and sea to create a highly appetizing and healthy cuisine.

WEDNESDAYS
10am – 2pm

Includes : All tuition, ingredients, use of all utensils and a free glass of wine with your meal

Not only will you learn how to cook the fabulous meals, but Katerina will also show you how to identify the wild mountain greens and *horta* that are used in the dishes.

Booking is essential

Four – Traditional Dips

TZATZIKI

A true Greek favourite that brings back memories of sitting under the infinite blue skies of Greece, relaxing and enjoying a glass of wine and a meal with friends.

It can be served as a dip for bread, or stuffed vine leaves (*dolmadakia*) or use it as a sauce for grilled meat dishes and souvlaki pitas.

INGREDIENTS

Serves approximately 6 people

2 ½ cups of strained yoghurt
1 teaspoon salt
1 large cucumber, unpeeled
    (or 2 medium size cucumbers, unpeeled)
2 garlic cloves
1 small carrot
4 tablespoons of Olive Oil
1 tablespoon white wine vinegar

PREPARATION

1. Grate the unpeeled cucumbers into a bowl and sprinkle with salt. Leave while you prepare the next step.

2. Mash the garlic cloves and place in a bowl with the yoghurt, olive oil and vinegar. Blend with a fork for a few minutes to mix the ingredients together. Let stand and go to step 3.

3. Taking a handful of the grated cucumber, squeeze to remove the water and place the cucumber in the bowl with the mix in step2. Repeat until all cucumber has been prepared in this way and is in the bowl.

You can dispose of the water, it is not needed.

4. Finely grate the carrot and stir into the mix.

5. Stir the mixture well until all the ingredients are blended.

6. Chill and serve in small bowls.

MELITZANOSALATA – Aubergine Dip

A wonderful dip that is full of flavour and so easy to make. Do not be tempted to rush the roasting process as it can make the aubergines a little bitter. It is better to wait another few minutes and do as the Cretans do… sit back and relax.

This is wonderful served with some fresh bread as part of a meze meal or as a side to meat dishes.

INGREDIENTS

4 Large Aubergines
1 Lemon
3 Cloves of Garlic
Olive Oil

Salt and Pepper
A Handful of Parsley

PREPARATION

1. Wash the aubergines and bake in a hot oven (200 C) for one hour until soft.

2. Allow to cool slightly before slicing them open and scooping out the insides into a large bowl. Discard the skins.

3. Peel and add the garlic cloves.

4. In batches, blend the above mixture adding the parsley, juice from the lemon and olive oil until it is a nice smooth consistency. Add salt and pepper to taste and mix in.

5. Cover the bowl with cling-film and place in the fridge for at least 30 minutes.

6. Just prior to serving, mix in a spoonful of mayonnaise for an extra creamy flavor and texture.

7. Serve in small bowls with bread or fresh, crunchy vegetables.

SKORDALIA – Garlic Dip

A tasty garlic dip that is wonderful as a dip with bread or fresh vegetables and also perfectly complements fried vegetables and meats. The best thing about this recipe is that it is so quick, easy and best of all…TASTY.

INGREDIENTS

1Kg Potatoes
8 Cloves Garlic
Teaspoon Salt
125ml Olive Oil
4 Tablespoons Lemon Juice

PREPARATION

1. Peel and boil the potatoes until soft.

2. Before they go completely cold, add them together with the rest of the ingredients into a large bowl.

3. Mash until a creamy consistency.

4. If required you can add chopped almonds or walnuts to add a little colour.

5. Serve as a dip with bread or fresh vegetables.

Cooking With Katerina

HOUMOUS or *HUMMUS* – Chick-pea Puree

A starter that everyone knows and loves, full of flavour and a traditional dish with all the tastes of the eastern Mediterranean.

INGREDIENTS

250g Chick Peas
2 Garlic Cloves
3 Tablespoons Olive Oil
3 Tablespoons Tahini (Sesame Seed Paste)
3 Tablespoons Lemon Juice
1 Teaspoon Salt
½ Teaspoon Pepper
1 Teaspoon Paprika

PREPARATION

1. Soak chick peas for at least 12 hours in water.

2. Replace the water and boil the chick peas until soft, then drain and allow them to cool for 10 minutes.

3. Mix the tahini paste in 2 dessert spoons of water to create a fluid mixture.

4. Add chick-peas to a blender and as it reduces down add the tahini mixture, salt, garlic, olive oil, pepper, paprika and lemon juice until the consistency is smooth and creamy.

5. Serve with bread or fresh, crunchy vegetables. It can be chilled and kept for up to seven days

FAVA – Split-Pea Dip

A simple yet filling dip or appetizer originally from the island of Santorini. It has spread to become a well known Greek dish throughout the world. Fava is normally cooled before serving but try it straight from the pan when still warm for a great winter snack.

INGREDIENTS

2 Cups Yellow Split Peas
500ml Olive Oil
1 Green Pepper
1 Large Red Onion
2 Cloves Garlic
1 Tomato
Salt/Pepper
1 Litre Water
Bay Leaf

PREPARATION

1. Place a litre of water and the split peas in a saucepan to boil.

2. Roughly chop the pepper, tomato, onion and the two garlic cloves and add to the water.

3. Add 2 teaspoons of salt, a pinch of pepper and the bay leaf.

4. Finally add the 500ml of olive oil and bring to a boil for 40 minutes.

5. After 40 minutes turn down the heat and simmer for an additional 30 minutes.

6. Remove from the heat and take out the bay leaf.

7. Blend the ingredients to a smooth consistency.

8. Chill in a fridge for at least an hour before serving.

It will keep for up to 7 days in the fridge.

KOKKINOYOULIA YIA SALATA – Beetroot Salad

A colourful addition to any table, this beetroot dip is as tasty as it is beautiful to look at with an array of textures that gives it a great crunch. It will keep for up to a week in the fridge.

INGREDIENTS

2Kg Plain Greek Yoghurt
200g Mayonnaise
1 Jar Pickled Beetroot *or* 800g Fresh Beetroot
125ml Olive oil
50ml Vinegar
4 Cloves Garlic
1 Cup Parsley
100g Chopped Walnuts

PREPARATION

1. Chop the beetroot into small and medium sized pieces. If using fresh beetroot it must be cooked before use by boiling to soften them.

2. Allow the beetroot to drain to remove any excess liquid.

3. In a large bowl add the yoghurt, mayonnaise and 50g of the walnuts.

4. Make a vinaigrette by mixing 125ml olive oil, 50ml vinegar and 2 cloves of chopped garlic and add to the yoghurt.

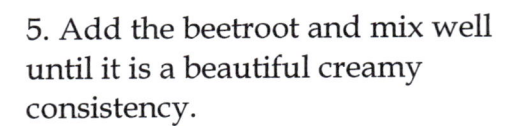

5. Add the beetroot and mix well until it is a beautiful creamy consistency.

6. Cover with cling film and chill for at least 1 hour in a fridge.

7. Serve chilled with bread or fresh, crunchy vegetables.

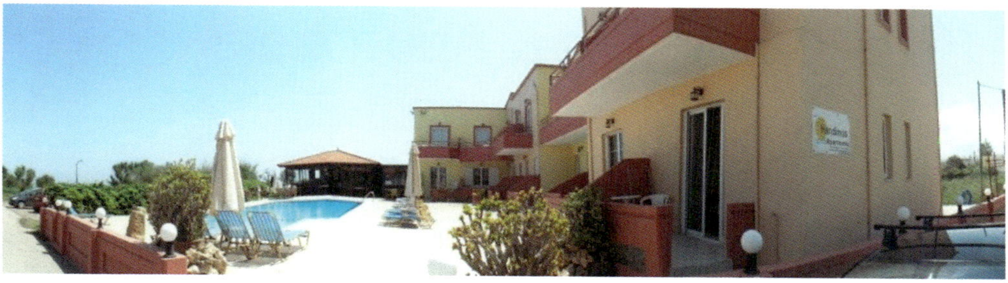

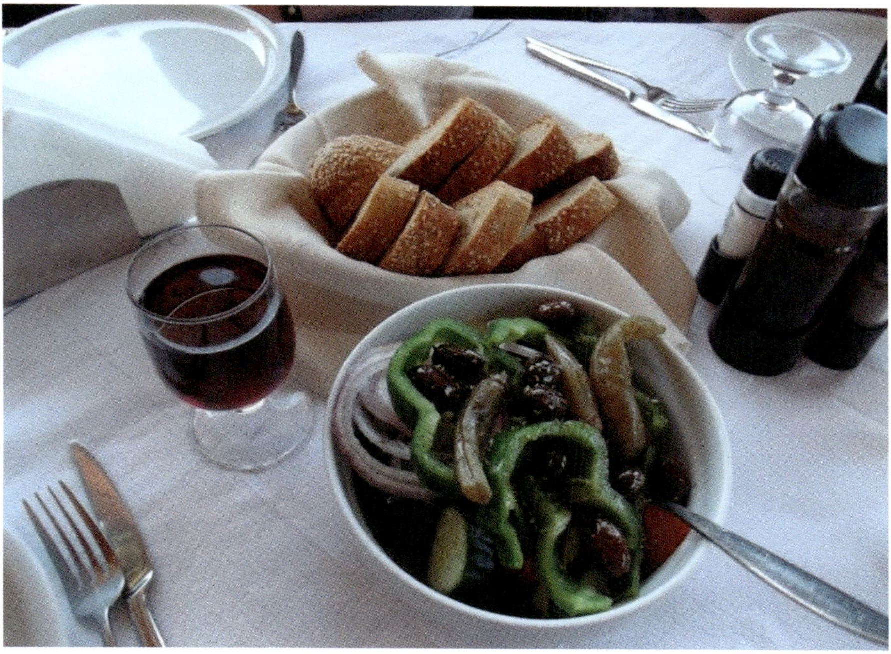

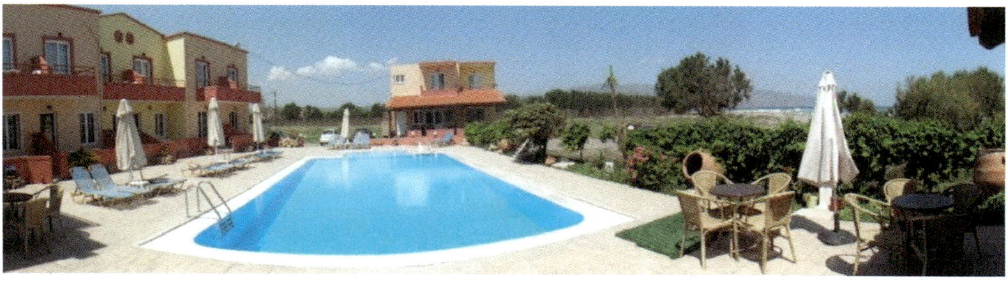

Five – Starters & Appetizers

GIGANTES – Butter Beans

A warming and hearty starter or main dish that is a firm favourite with everyone. Once you have soaked the beans it is quick and easy to make and a true Cretan recipe.

INGREDIENTS

½ Kilo Butter Beans (Gigantes)
2 Large Tomatoes
1 Red Onion
1 Clove of Garlic
1 Carrot
250g Tomato Passata
Olive Oil
Small Glass of Red Wine

Handful of Fresh Parsley
Salt / Pepper

PREPARATION

1. Soak the beans overnight in water.

2. Drain the beans and discard the water.

3. In a pressure cooker cook the beans for 10 minutes, or boil in a saucepan for approximately 1 hour until soft.

4. Blend the tomatoes, onion and garlic until a smooth liquid.

5. In a large flat oven dish pour in 2 tablespoons of olive oil and spread around the base.

6. Add the blended ingredients and the beans to the pan.

7. Add a handful of chopped parsley.

8. Peel and slice the carrot and add to the pan.

9. Add 2 teaspoons of salt, 1 teaspoon of pepper, a litre of water and the glass of red wine and stir until well mixed.

10. Place pan in a hot oven and cook at 200 C for 1 hour 15 minutes.

11. Serve with bread and if you wish to add a creamy flavour, crumble some feta cheese over the top.

KOLOKITHOKEFTEDES - Fried Zucchini Balls

When courgettes are in season there are just so many that you need many different ways to cook them. This KOLOKITHOKEFTEDES recipe is a great way to use up your spare courgettes in a delicious and quick way.

INGREDIENTS (FOR 8 – 10 PEOPLE)

4 Large Courgettes
500g Feta Cheese
1 Red Onion
250g Grated Regatto Cheese
250g Bread Crumbs
200g Plain Flour

Cooking With Katerina

½ Cup Fresh or Dried Mint
Oregano
Pepper
Salt

PREPARATION

1. Grate your courgettes into a colander that is sitting over an empty bowl.

2. Sprinkle salt over the courgettes and mix together by hand.

3. Leave for 20 minutes to allow the water to drain from the grated courgettes.

4. Once drained take a handful of the courgette and squeeze to remove any excess water before placing them in a clean bowl.
*** TOP TIP – EXCESS WATER WILL MAKE YOUR COURGETTE BALLS FALL APART WHEN COOKED ***

5. Blend the onion and add to the bowl.

6. Finely chop the mint and add to the bowl.

7. Add 2 teaspoons of salt, 1 teaspoon of pepper and 1 teaspoon of oregano.

8. Crumble the feta into the bowl and also add the regatto cheese and breadcrumbs.

9. Mix by hand until well blended together and of a firm consistency. It should begin to stick together and form a solid mix.

10. Press down firmly on the mix with the heel of your palm and cover the bowl with cling film. Leave to one side for 10 – 15 minutes.

11. Place the plain flour in a small bowl. This will be used to coat your courgette balls before frying.

12. Take a handful of the courgette mix and shape into a flattened ball.

13. Dip the ball into the flour to coat the external surface.

14. Deep fry in small batches and allow to cool before serving.

MARATHO PITES – Fennel Pies

Made with wild fennel picked fresh from the olive groves, this is a wonderfully simple yet tasty and filling snack.

INGREDIENTS – Makes 10 -12 pies

Filling
500g Fresh Fennel Fronds
200g Spring Onion Stems
1 Large Onion
250g Spinach
4 Cloves Garlic
200g Plain Flour
125ml Olive Oil
Salt/Pepper
Cumin

Pastry
500ml Warm Water
Teaspoon Yeast
25ml Raki (Tsikoudia)
25ml Olive Oil
1Kg All Purpose Flour
Salt

PREPARATION

1. Dissolve the yeast in the warm water adding the raki, olive oil and 2 dessert spoons of salt.

2. Slowly stir in 1Kg of all purpose flour to make the dough. If it is too wet add more flour a little at a time, too dry just add a little water. It should be elastic and not stick to your hands when of the right consistency. Do not overwork the dough by kneading it softly.

3. Place the dough in a clean plastic bag and leave in a warm place to rest for at least 30 minutes.

4. For the filling, finely chop the fennel, spring onions, large onion, spinach and garlic and place in a large mixing bowl.

5. Add 125ml of olive oil, a teaspoon of cumin, 2 dessert spoons of salt and 1 dessert spoon of pepper.

6. Thoroughly mix this together and leave to stand for 10 minutes. This allows the excess water to drain to the bottom of the bowl.

Cooking With Katerina

7. Drain the water from the bowl and squeeze the mixture to extract as much liquid as possible.

8. Add 200g of plain flour to bind your mixture together.

9. After your dough has rested, cut and roll it into fist sized balls on a floured surface.

10. Spread out the dough ball with your hands and place a ball of your filling into the centre.

11. Fold the edges of your dough over the filling and squeeze them together to form a seal.

12. Leave to rest for 10 minutes before gently rolling out your dough balls with a rolling pin into a thin round sheet.

13. If you have made too many this is an ideal time to freeze them, placing a sheet of greaseproof paper between each pie.

14. To cook, fry in hot oil for a few minutes on each side and serve either hot or cold.

SFAKIAN PIE – Cheese Pie with honey

A delicious specialty of North-West Crete with a filling of myzithra cheese that is traditional drizzled with honey. They an be served as a filling snack, appetizer or even as dessert.

INGREDIENTS – Makes approx 15 pies

1kg Myzithra Cheese
500ml Warm Water
Teaspoon Yeast
25ml Raki (Tsikoudia)
25ml Olive Oil
1Kg All Purpose Flour
Salt

PREPARATION

1. Dissolve the yeast in the warm water adding the raki, olive oil and 2 dessert spoons of salt.

2. Slowly stir in 1Kg of all purpose flour to make the dough. If it is too wet add more flour a little at a time, too dry just add a little water.
It should be elastic and not stick to your hands when of the right consistency. Do not overwork the dough by kneading it softly.

3. Place the dough in a clean plastic bag and leave in a warm place to rest for at least 30 minutes.

4. Roll the cheese into palm sized balls.

5. After your dough has rested, cut and roll it into fist sized balls on a floured surface.

6. Spread out the dough ball with your hands and place a ball of cheese into the centre.

7. Fold the edges of your dough over the filling and squeeze them together to form a seal.

8. Leave to rest for 10 minutes before gently rolling out your dough balls with a rolling pin into a thin round sheet.

9. If you have made too many this is an ideal time to freeze them, placing a sheet of greaseproof paper between each pie.

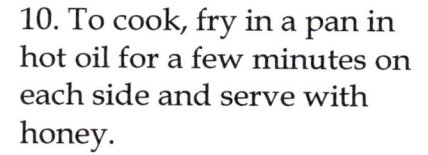

10. To cook, fry in a pan in hot oil for a few minutes on each side and serve with honey.

Cooking With Katerina

SAGANAKI TYRI – Fried Cheese

A rich, filling treat where you try not to think of the calories you are about to consume. Sprinkled with lemon juice and served hot, Saganaki Tyri is a delicious and hearty snack.

INGREDIENTS

Slices of Saganaki Cheese
Flour

PREPARATION

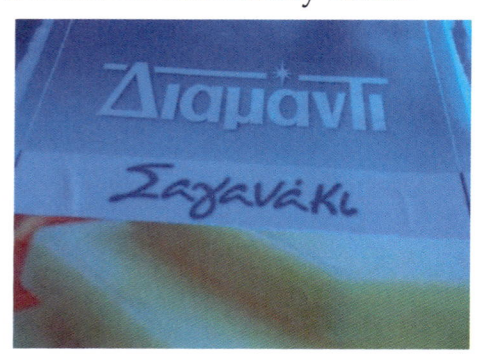

1. If your cheese is not already cut, slice into 1cm thick pieces.

2. Run the slices under a running tap for a few seconds before coating with flour.

3. Heat oil in a frying pan until very hot and then place a slice of your flour coated cheese into the pan. The oil should reach about half way up the cheese slice.

4. Turn your saganaki after a minute or when it turns a lovely golden brown colour.

5. Once cooked on both sides, serve while still warm with half a lemon.

PATATES KEFTEDES – Fried Potato Balls

Crisp, delicious potato balls with a soft, fluffy centre. These are perfect as an appetizer or as a side dish for a main meal.

INGREDIENTS – for 60-70 fried balls

1Kg Potatoes
200g Butter
500g Grated Edam Cheese
1 Finely Chopped Onion
200g Chopped Spring Onion
1 Cup Finely Chopped Parsley
1 Cup Finely Chopped Mint
2 Cups Fine Breadcrumbs
4 Eggs
Salt/Pepper
Packet of Herb Mix for Salad

Herb Mix

PREPARATION

1. Peel the potatoes and place in a pan of water with 2 dessert spoons of salt and bring to the boil until soft.

2. Mash your boiled potatoes adding 200g of butter and 2 tablespoons of salt for taste.

3. Whilst mashing, add 2 dessert spoons black pepper, the onion, herb mix and spring onions.

4. Now add 500g grated Edam cheese and 4 eggs (beaten) to the potato and mix well together.

5. Leave the mixture to cool for 10-15 minutes.

6. Lightly flour a baking tray and roll out small balls of your mix, covering them with the flour in your baking tray. The balls can be frozen at this point, if you have made too many, for cooking at a later date.

7. Deep fry the balls until golden brown and crispy. Drain on kitchen towel before serving.

DOLMADAKIA – Stuffed Vine Leaves

Dolmadakia can be made with either a meat or vegetarian filling according to your preference. Serve with a bowl of tzatziki and enjoy the flavours of Crete.

INGREDIENTS

500g Fresh, Canned or Frozen Vine Leaves
4 Large Tomatoes
1 Large Onion
1 Clove Garlic
Cup of Fennel
Cup of Parsley
½ Cup of Mint
250g Rice
250ml Tomato Passata
Tomato Paste

500ml Olive Oil
250ml Water
Salt/Pepper
Cumin
500g Minced Beef (If Required)

PREPARATION

1. Blanch your vine leaves in boiling water for 2 minutes to soften them.

2. Blend together 4 tomatoes, 1 onion, 1 clove garlic along with the fennel, parsley and mint and place in a large bowl.

3. Add the rice, tomato passata, a dessert spoon of tomato paste and 250ml of olive oil. Mix the contents together with your hands to fully blend the ingredients together.

(You can add the mince beef at this point if required.)

4. Place a vine leaf, with the veins facing upwards in your hand and place a heap of the mixture in the centre.

5. Fold over the edges of the leaf and roll up to seal the contents within the vine leaf. Place in an oven dish. Repeat until you have used all of the vine leaves or all of the mixture.

6. Pour the remaining olive oil and sprinkle 250ml water over the vine leaves in your oven dish.

7. Cook in a pre-heated oven at 220 C for 45mins to an hour. Test one of your dolmadakia to ensure the rice is soft and cooked before serving.

8. Serve hot or cold with a side dish of tzatziki or as part of a delicious meze.

FASOLADA – Bean Soup

Perfect for a cold winter's day after a morning spent working outside, Fasolada is a tasty bean soup that uses all the freshest ingredients of the winter garden. A delicious starter or main course that is quick and simple to make.

INGREDIENTS

500g Dried Beans (Your choice of beans)
2 Carrots (Sliced)
1 Cup Celery (Roughly Chopped)
2 Large Onions (Roughly Chopped)
1 Clove Garlic (Sliced)
500g Tomato Passata
2 Bay Leaves
Salt/Pepper

PREPARATION

1. Place the beans in a pressure cooker and just cover in cold water.

2. Cook for 20 minutes then drain and discard the water.

3. Add 500ml olive oil to the beans along with the rest of the ingredients.

4. Add 1.25 litres of cold water and cook for a further 30 minutes in the pressure cooker.

5. Serve hot with bread.

ALMYRO ZAMBON KAI TYRI TOURTA –

Salty ham and cheese cake

A savoury cake that is a wonderful appetizer. It can be made without the ham for your vegetarian guests.

INGREDIENTS – Enough for 5 medium cakes

250g Butter
5 Eggs
500ml Milk
750g Plain Flour
40g Baking Powder
400g Grated Cheese (of your choice)
400g Ham or Bacon or Spam

PREPARATION

1. Separate the yolks from the whites of your eggs, keep the whites to one side for later use.

2. Add 250g of melted butter to the egg yolks and slowly whisk in 500ml of milk.

3. Add the flour and baking powder slowly as you whisk the dough until it is just thick enough not to drip off the whisk.

4. Gently whisk the egg whites and add to the dough.

5. Add 400g of grated cheese and mix in gently.
If you are making your cake without the ham proceed to Step 7

6. Add your chopped ham/bacon/spam to the dough and mix in.

7. Grease a cake tin with sunflower oil and half fill the tin with your dough mix to allow it to rise during baking.

8. Bake at 175 C for 45 minutes and allow to cool before serving.

Six – Main Courses

BOUREKI

A true Cretan specialty originally from the region of Chania where it is sometimes made without the pastry base and topping. Either way, it is a delicious dish that makes full use of the glut of courgettes and potatoes that abound in the summer garden.

It freezes well and there will not be a household on Crete that will not have a boureki in their freezer ready for a quick meal.

INGREDIENTS

½ Kilo of Potatoes
½ Kilo of Courgettes
125g Malaka Cheese (A soft cheese similar to Mozzarella)
250g Mizythra Cheese (A creamy, crumbly goats cheese)
750g Plain Flour
15g Fresh Yeast (Dried yeast can also be used)
250ml Sunflower Oil
500ml Milk
Handful of Fresh Mint Leaves (Dried can be used)
Sesame Seeds
Salt / Pepper
Olive Oil

PREPARATION

First you need to prepare the pastry dough as you need to put it to rest to one side whilst you make the boureki filling.

1. In a large bowl add 250ml warm milk to the yeast and stir gently until the yeast has dissolved.

2. Add the sunflower oil to the milk and yeast with a pinch of salt.

3. Stir in 500g of plain flour using your hands to mix and knead the ingredients until a dough like consistency is reached.

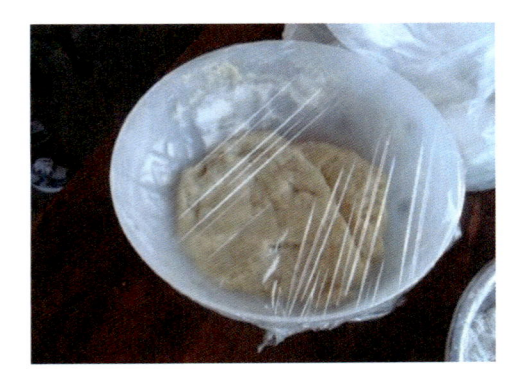

4. Cover the bowl with cling-film and a towel and place in a warm area to rest.

5. To make the boureki filling, slice the courgettes and potatoes into a large bowl using a mandolin.

6. Add the Malaka and Mizythra cheese.

7. Finely chop the mint leaves and add to the mix along with 2 tablespoons of salt and 1 tablespoon of pepper.

8. Add 2 tablespoons of plain flour and mix the contents of the bowl vigorously by hand until all ingredients are well mixed together.

9. In a large square oven pan pour two tablespoons of olive oil and ensure the bottom of the pan and part of the sides are well greased.

10. Remove half of the pastry and roll out with a little flour to avoid it sticking until it will fit into the bottom of your pan.

11. Pour the boureki mix over the pastry lined oven pan and smooth out with your hand to avoid too much unevenness.

12. Roll out the remaining pastry and place over the mix, folding and flattening the edges to fully cover the boureki filling.

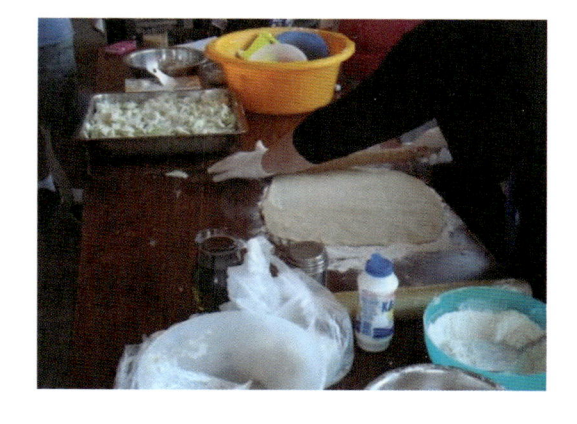

13. Use a large knife to cut the boureki into serving sized portions ensuring you cut all the way through the top and bottom layers of pastry.

14. Pour over 250ml of olive oil and 250ml of milk.

15. Sprinkle a handful of sesame seeds over the top of your boureki.

16. Place in a hot oven (200 C) for 1 ½ to 2 hours ensuring you cover your dish with foil after 30 minutes of cooking time.

17. Serve whilst hot.

MOUSSAKA

No Cretan recipe book would be complete without the wonderful Moussaka. Layers of mince-meat, aubergine, potatoes and a thick, creamy béchamel sauce that epitomizes the flavours of Greece.

INGREDIENTS – For 8 - 10 generous servings

4 Large Aubergines
4 Large Potatoes
500g Minced Beef
2 Large Onions
2 Cloves Garlic
250g Regatto Cheese (Grated)
200ml Olive Oil
A Bay Leaf
Dried Peel from half an Orange

Cinnamon Stick
1 Bay Leaf
Large Glass of Red Wine
Salt/Pepper

FOR THE BECHAMEL SAUCE

1.5 Litres Milk
1 Egg
50g Butter
150g grated Edam
3 Dessert Spoons Corn Flour
Nutmeg
Salt

PREPARATION

1. Cut the aubergines lengthwise into 1-2cm thick slices and soak in cold water for 30 minutes.

2. Peel and slice the potatoes lengthways slightly thinner than that of the aubergines. This allows them to cook over the same time as the aubergines. Place to one side.

3. Add the olive oil to a large pan on a high heat before adding the mince beef.

4. Chop and dice the onions and add to the pan.

5. Slice or crush the garlic and add to the pan along with a teaspoon of salt and ½ teaspoon pepper.

6. Add the bay leaf, cinnamon stick, red wine and the dried orange peel to the pan and stir together.

7. Reduce the heat and simmer the bolognaise mix with the lid on for 20 minutes.

8. After soaking the aubergines, shallow fry until soft NOT browned. Repeat for the potato slices.

9. Grease an oven dish with olive oil and layer it with potatoes, bolognaise, aubergines and grated cheese until full or you run out of ingredients.
   **** ENSURE YOU HAVE REMOVED THE CINNAMON STICK, BAYLEAF AND ORANGE PEEL. ****

10. Finish the top layer with the bolognaise mix and leave to cool as you make the Béchamel Sauce.

11. To make your own Béchamel Sauce add 1 litre of milk and ½ teaspoon of grated nutmeg to a pan and bring to a slow boil.

12. In a jug, whisk 500 ml of cold milk with 1 egg, 1 teaspoon of salt and 3 dessert spoons of corn flour.

13. When the milk in the pan is boiling add the cold whisked contents slowly, stirring and mixing continuously.

14. Whisk in 50g of butter and 100g of grated Edam until thick and creamy.

15. Pour over the Moussaka layered dish and sprinkle 50g of grated Edam over the top.

16. Bake in an oven at 200 C for 20 minutes until topping is a nice golden brown colour.

YEMISTA – Stuffed Peppers and Tomato

Colourful, tasty and one of the most popular dishes of Greece. This recipe is based on the traditional method of stuffing the vegetables with rice and herbs, but why not experiment with minced meats or other fillings.

INGREDIENTS – For 4-6 servings

6 Large Green Peppers
6 Large Tomatoes
1 Large Onion
1 Clove Garlic
Cup of Fennel Fronds or Leaves
Cup of Parsley
½ Cup of Mint

1 Dessert Spoon Rice for each Vegetable
250ml Tomato Passata
Tomato Paste
500ml Olive Oil
250ml Water
Salt/Pepper
Ground Cumin

PREPARATION

TOP TIP – Cutting the bottoms off the peppers and tomatoes instead of the top will make them stand up better in your pan.

1. Cut off the bottoms of your peppers and tomatoes keeping the removed section for use later.

2. De-seed your vegetables being careful not to damage the skin and place the hollow vegetables into an oven dish.

3. Blend the tomato pulp in a bowl and keep as the basis for your stuffing.

4. Add the rice (1 dessert spoon for each vegetable), 250ml olive oil, 250ml of tomato passata and a dessert spoon of tomato paste to the bowl.

5. 'Finely chop all herbs and put in the bowl along with the finely chopped onion and garlic, 2 dessert spoons of salt, 1 teaspoon of pepper and a heaped teaspoon of cumin.

6. Mix the contents of the bowl together by hand to fully blend the ingredients.

7. Stuff the peppers and tomatoes with your mixture and seal with the cut off portion from Step 1. They should be standing up nicely in your oven dish.

8. Drizzle the remaining olive oil (250ml) over the stuffed vegetables and also sprinkle with 250ml water.

9. Cover the dish with foil and place in a pre-heated oven at 220 C for an hour.

10. After one hour, remove the foil and bake for another 20 minutes to brown the vegetables.

11. Serve hot or cold.

SOUTSOUKAKIA – Spiced Meat Balls

Lightly spiced to provide a little heat to the taste buds, this soutsoukakia dish is a filling meal for any time of the year. Cooked in a delicious tomato sauce that infuses the meat with a mouth watering flavour, the meatballs can be served with your choice of pasta, potatoes or rice.

INGREDIENTS

FOR THE MEATBALLS
1 Kilo Minced Beef
250g Bread
250ml Red Wine
2 Large Onions
1 Large Tomato

Olive Oil
Salt/ Pepper
Hot Paprika
Olive Oil
½ Cup of Mint Leaves

FOR THE SAUCE
500g Tomato Passata
250ml Red Wine
Cumin
2 Cloves Garlic
2 Tomatoes
1 Onion
Dessert Spoon Tomato Puree
Salt/Pepper

PREPARATION

1. Soak the bread in 250ml red wine until saturated.

2. Finely chop the mint and add to a bowl with the minced beef.

3. Squeeze out the bread to remove the excess wine and crumble into the bowl.

4. Add a tablespoon of olive oil, 2 teaspoons of pepper, 1 teaspoon of cumin, 3 teaspoons of salt and 1 heaped teaspoon of paprika.

5. Finely chop the onions and add to the mix.

6. Roughly chop the tomato and add.

7. Add the two eggs and blend the mixture by hand. Knead and press the blended mixture to form a semi firm texture at the bottom of the bowl.

8. Cover the bowl with cling film and leave the meat to rest as you prepare the sauce.

9. For the sauce; in a large saucepan on a medium heat, add 500ml olive oil, 2 minced cloves of garlic, 1 minced onion, 2 tablespoons of salt and 1 teaspoon of cumin.

10. Bring to a simmer and add 1 liter of water. Cover and leave to cook.

11. Place a sheet of greaseproof paper on an oven tray in preparation for the meatballs.

12. Using the mince meat mixture, shape an elongated ball in your hand, rolling the mix to ensure it is a firm yet not too dense texture and place on the baking tray.

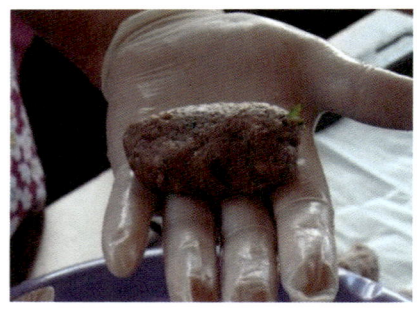

13. Repeat until you have the desired amount of meatballs or until the mince meat has been used up.

14. Place in a hot oven at 200 C for one hour.

15. Once the meatballs have cooked place them in your saucepan of simmering sauce and leave for 15-20 minutes.

16. Serve hot with rice, potatoes or pasta.

BRIAM – Traditional Vegetarian Dish

A hearty and delicious dish that makes use of the finest, fresh vegetables that Crete has to offer. Full of flavour, it is a warming meal on a cold winter day.

INGREDIENTS – for 6-8 people

500ml Olive Oil
1 Large Red Onion
5 Cloves of Garlic
2 Red Peppers
2 Green Peppers
2 Carrots
3 Aubergines
3 Potatoes (peeled)
3 Courgettes

2 Ripe Tomatoes
Handful of Fresh Parsley
500ml Tomato Passata
Regatto Cheese (grated)
Salt/Pepper

PREPARATION

1. Add 500ml olive oil to a large saucepan.

2. Roughly chop all the vegetables and add to the pan ensuring you deseed the peppers.

3. Add 3 dessert spoons of salt and 2 dessert spoons of pepper.

4. Place on a high heat with the lid on and leave for 5 minutes.

5. Agitate the pan, leaving the lid on, to slightly mix the contents and leave for a further 5 minutes.

6. Stir the contents and mix in the 500ml passata and 125ml of cold water.

7. Leave to cook with the lid on for 20 minutes.

8. Prior to serving sprinkle the top with grated regatto cheese and serve hot.

Cooking With Katerina

STIFADO – Beef or Rabbit in red wine sauce

The aromas that drift through your kitchen as this stifado cooks will have your taste buds tingling long before it is ready to eat. One of the most well known and well loved dishes of Greece, it is a must have in any recipe book. Made with a hint of cinnamon that helps to bring out the exquisite flavours of the meat, Katerina's easy recipe for stifado is guaranteed to satisfy many hungry mouths.

INGREDIENTS

1kg of Beef or Rabbit
500ml Olive oil
3 Large Red Onions
500g Small White Onions (Silverskin Onions)
5 Cloves Garlic
500ml Tomato Passata

250ml Red Wine
Cinnamon Stick
2 Bay Leaves
1 Dessert Spoon Whole Black Peppercorns
Salt/Pepper

PREPARATION

1. Cube the beef or cut the rabbit into large pieces and place in a large saucepan.

2. Just cover the meat with coldwater and simmer on a low-medium heat for 15 minutes.

3. Whilst the meat is simmering, prepare your vegetables by roughly chopping the 3 large onions and 5 cloves of garlic.

4. Drain off and discard the water from the meat once it has simmered for the 15 minutes and add 500ml of olive oil, 2 dessert spoons of salt, 1 dessert spoon of pepper and the chopped onions and garlic.

5. Add the cinnamon stick, a scattering of whole peppercorns and the 2 bay leaves and stir the contents of the pan before placing back on the heat.

6. Leave to cook for 15 minutes, stirring occasionally.

7. Add the 500ml tomato passata, 500ml water, 250ml red wine and 500g of small white onions.

8. Mix the contents together and bring back to a boil.

9. Leave to cook for 30 minutes and the liquid has reduced down to a rich juice. Remove the bay leaves and cinnamon stick.

10. Serve hot with potatoes, rice or pasta.

KLEFTIKO – *Hidden Meat* Pie

Traditionally made in a pit that is dug in the ground, Kleftiko was a way of cooking meat which gave off hardly any cooking aromas. This was a useful thing when you are living in the mountains with *Brigands* and hiding out from the invading Turks. The modern day version is cooked in pastry to simulate the earth, but it is still just as tasty today as it was over a hundred years ago.

INGREDIENTS

1.5Kg Boneless Leg of Lamb
2 Large Onions (Chopped)
4 Peeled Potatoes
250g Peas
250g Chopped Carrots

250ml White Wine
250ml Olive Oil
100g Grated Edam Cheese
6 Cloves of Garlic (Roughly Chopped)
1 Dessert Spoon Mint (Dried and Chopped)
Salt/Pepper

PASTRY
15g Yeast
1 Glass (250ml) Milk
1 Glass (250ml) Olive Oil
1 Egg
1Kg Plain Flour
1 Dessert Spoon Salt

PREPARATION

1. Make the pastry first to give it time to rest as you make the kleftiko filling. In a large bowl add 250ml warm milk to the yeast and stir gently until the yeast has dissolved.

2. Add the olive oil to the milk and yeast with a pinch of salt.

3. Stir in 1Kg of plain flour using your hands to mix and knead the ingredients until a dough like consistency is reached.

4. Cover the bowl with cling-film and a towel and place in a warm area to rest.

5. Add the olive oil, chopped onions and garlic to a pan and place on a high heat.

6. Add 2 dessert spoons of salt and 1 dessert spoon of pepper.

7. Roughly cut the lamb into small pieces and add to the pan, stirring the contents well.

8. Chop your potatoes to the same size as your lamb pieces and add to the pan along with the peas and carrots.

9. Cook through for 10 minutes until the potatoes have softened slightly then remove from the heat.

10. You can make kleftiko in various ways; as individual pots, in a large oven pan or as a wrapped pie (*pasty in the UK*). It is up to you how you utilize your pastry and filling, remember that individual pots do not require pastry along the bottom of the pot.

IN AN OVEN PAN
11. For a large group of people use a deep oven pan and layer with a sheet of rolled out pastry.

12. Lay out your filling in an even layer atop this pastry bottom. Sprinkle with grated Edam cheese.

13. Using another sheet of pastry the same size as your base, place it on top of your filling and gently press the edges down around the sides.

14. Brush with a beaten egg and sprinkle with sesame seeds before placing in a hot oven at 200 C for 30-40 minutes and the pastry is a deep golden brown.

15. Cut into portions and serve.

INDIVIDUAL PIES (or Pasties)
16. Roll out a sheet of pastry to a rough circular shape.

17. Place a large spoonful of your filling in the centre of your pastry circle.

18. Fold over the pastry and squeeze the edges together to form a seal.

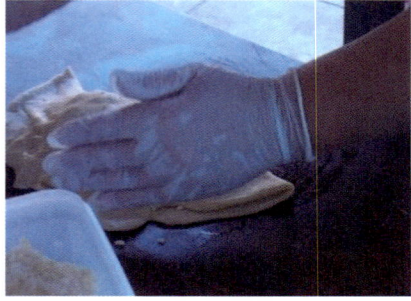

19. Brush with a beaten egg and sprinkle with sesame seeds before placing in a hot oven at 200 C for 30 minutes and the pastry has turned a lovely golden colour.

20. Serve hot or cold.

BAKALAOS – Cod with Garlic

Chunks of crispy fried cod with a side of garlic mash that will have everybody asking for more. If using salted cod remember to soak it overnight, refreshing the water 3-4 times to remove the salt.

INGREDIENTS

1Kg Boned Cod Pieces
250g Plain Flour
Oregano
Baking Powder
Salt/Pepper

For The Skordalia
1Kg Potatoes

8 Cloves Garlic
1 Teaspoon Salt
125ml Olive Oil
4 Tablespoons Lemon Juice (or vinegar if wanting a sharper flavour with the cod)

PREPARATION

For The Skordalia
1. Peel and boil the potatoes until soft.

2. Before they go completely cold mash them together with the rest of the ingredients.

3. Mash until a smooth consistency and place to one side as you prepare the cod.

4. In a mixing bowl add a tablespoon of each of the oregano, salt and pepper along with a teaspoon of baking powder.

5. Add the flour and mix well.

6. When deep frying your cod you must ensure that the oil is hot before you place in the cod pieces.

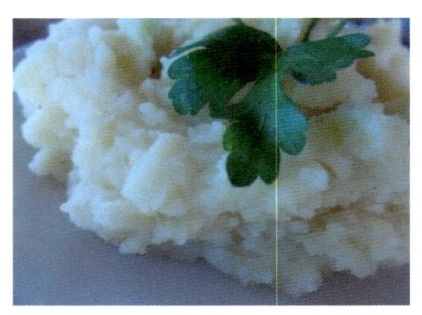

7. Dip and roll your cod pieces in the flour mixture and place in the hot oil for 4-5 minutes and they have become a light golden colour.

8. Serve immediately with the garlic mash as a side dish.

IMAM BALDI – Stuffed Aubergines

Imam Baldi literally means, 'The Imam Faints'. The story behind the dish is that one day the Imam's wife prepared him this meal and he fainted with pleasure upon the taste. Another version of events is that he fainted when he realised just how much olive oil had gone into the dish, which at that time was a very expensive commodity. Either way it is a dish that tastes delicious.

INGREDIENTS

8 Aubergines (1 per serving)
500ml Olive Oil

3 Large Onions
5 Cloves Garlic
4 Large, Ripe Tomatoes
500ml Tomato Passata
50ml Red Wine
500g Feta Cheese
1 Cup Mint
1 Cup Parsley
½ Cup Basil
1 Tablespoon Black Peppercorns
Bay Leaf

PREPARATION

1. Remove the stems from the aubergines and cut a thin strip of the flesh from each side.

2. In the centre of one of the strips, cut a slit lengthways into the centre of the aubergine.

3. Soak the aubergines in salted water for 30 minutes. This helps to sweeten them.

4. Remove from the water and leave on a cloth to dry for 15-20 minutes. Pat with the towel to remove any excess water before frying.

Cooking With Katerina

5. Deep fry the aubergines in hot oil until they have softened and turned brown in colour. Leave to drain in a colander over a shallow bowl as you prepare the filling.

6. Finely chop the 3 onions and 5 cloves of garlic and add to a pan with 500ml olive oil and a dessert spoon of salt. Fry until the onions are softened.

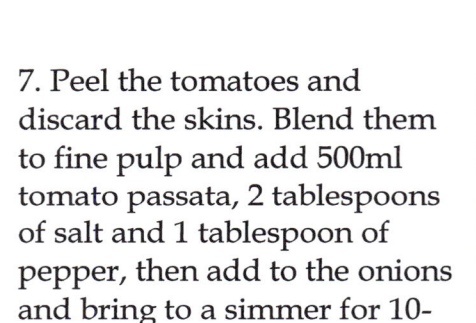

7. Peel the tomatoes and discard the skins. Blend them to fine pulp and add 500ml tomato passata, 2 tablespoons of salt and 1 tablespoon of pepper, then add to the onions and bring to a simmer for 10-15minutes.

8. Add the chopped basil, parsley and mint.

9. Add 50ml of red wine, a whole bay leaf and a tablespoon of black peppercorns.

10. Bring back to the simmer before removing from the heat.

11. Place your drained aubergines in a shallow oven pan with the slits towards the top. Use a spoon to stuff the aubergines with the ingredients from your pan. Any sauce left over can be jarred or frozen for later use.

12. Add a piece of feta cheese to each aubergine to add a creamy taste.

13. Bake the aubergines in an oven at 200 C for 40 minutes.

14. Sprinkle with grated cheese prior to serving.

SOUPIA – Cuttlefish in Red Wine Sauce

A delicious red wine stock gives this dish a rich flavour that works well with the cuttlefish. If you have never cooked cuttlefish before then this simple but delicious recipe will tempt you to try it again and again.

INGREDIENTS

1Kg Fresh or Frozen Cuttlefish
250ml Olive Oil
2 Large Onions
5 Cloves Garlic
2 Large Ripe Tomatoes
2 Deseeded Green Peppers
200g Spring Onions
2 Carrots
1 Cup Parsley
1 Cup Mint
125ml Red Wine

500g Tomato Passata
Salt/Pepper

PREPARATION

1. Clean and boil the cuttlefish for 10 minutes until softened.

2. Drain the water and chop the cuttlefish into large pieces before placing in a saucepan.

3. Roughly chop the onions, Garlic and tomatoes and add to the pan with 250ml olive oil.

4. Finely chop the parsley, mint and spring onions and add to the pan along with 2 dessert spoons of salt and 1 dessert spoon of pepper.

5. Place the pan on a medium heat for 10 minutes to cook through softly, stirring occasionally.

6. Now add 125ml of red wine, 500ml tomato passata and 1 ½ litres of cold water and bring to a simmer for 20 minutes.

7. Thinly slice the carrots, roughly chop the green peppers and add to the pan.

8. Cook for a further 10 minutes and serve.

PASTITSIO

Layers of spaghetti pasta and juicy minced beef in a rich tomato and red wine sauce topped off with a creamy homemade béchamel sauce that is baked in the oven. Delicious!

INGREDIENTS – Enough for 10 very generous portions

500g Spaghetti (Size No. 3)
1.5 Kg Minced Beef
500ml Olive Oil
2 Large Onions
2 Cloves Garlic
500g Tomato Passata
4 Eggs
400g Grated Regatto Cheese
250ml Red Wine

3 Bay leaves
Cinnamon Stick
Salt/Pepper

FOR THE BECHAMEL SAUCE
1.5 Litres Milk
1 Egg
50g Butter
150g grated Edam
3 Dessert Spoons Corn Flour
Nutmeg
Salt

PREPARATION

1. Cook the spaghetti for 5-10 minutes until al dente and leave to one side.

2. In a large saucepan add 500ml olive oil and the minced beef and place on a low heat.

3. Roughly chop the onions and garlic and add to the pan along with 3 dessert spoons of salt, 1 dessert spoon of black pepper, a cinnamon stick and 3 bay leaves.

4. Mix the contents together and cook for 10 minutes with the lid on.

5. Add 250ml red wine, 500g tomato passata and 250ml water. Stir and leave the pastistio filling to cook for 30 minutes.

Cooking With Katerina

6. Grease a large oven dish with sunflower oil and add the pasta. Sprinkle most of your grated regatto cheese over the pasta, leaving a handful for later. Mix the pasta and cheese together.

7. Separate the egg whites and whisk to a frothy meringue before mixing into the pasta and cheese. This adds lightness to the dish.

8. Make your béchamel sauce by placing 1 litre of milk and ½ teaspoon of grated nutmeg to a pan and bring to a slow boil.

9. In a jug, whisk 500 ml of cold milk with 1 egg, 1 teaspoon of salt and 3 dessert spoons of corn flour.

10. When the milk in the pan is boiling add the cold whisked contents slowly, stirring and mixing continuously.

11. Whisk in 50g of butter and 100g of grated Edam until thick and creamy.

12. Trying to leave as much of the oil in the saucepan as possible, start spooning your pastitsio filling over the pasta, mixing it in as you go.

13. Once the filling is in, pour over your béchamel sauce and sprinkle the last of your grated regatto cheese over the top.

14. Bake in an oven at 200 C for 45 minutes and serve.

Seven – Desserts

LOUKOUMADES – Fried Honey Balls

Perfect for those with a sweet tooth, loukoumades are simple and quick to make and a great favourite to finish off a meal. They especially go well with a glass of tsikoudia (raki) or two! The recipe will make approximately 100 loukoumades.

INGREDIENTS

15g Dried Yeast *or* 2cm cube of Fresh Yeast

½ Kilo of All Purpose Flour

Salt

500ml Warm Water

Sesame Seeds

Cinnamon Powder

FOR SYRUP

1 Kilo Sugar

500ml Water

A Large Lemon

Honey

PREPARATION

1. In a large bowl dissolve the yeast in the warm water.

2. Slowly add the flour and a teaspoon of salt, mixing with your hands until it is of a smooth and paste like consistency.

3. Cover with cling-film and a towel and leave to rest at room temperature for around 1 hour.

4. Whilst the dough is resting you can make the syrup.

5. MAKING THE SYRUP - Add the sugar and water to a pan and place on a medium heat to dissolve the sugar completely. Stir frequently and ensure it does not come to the boil.

6. Add a dessert spoon of honey to the sugar syrup and stir in.

7. Add the juice from a quarter of the lemon and stir in.

8. The correct consistency is met when the liquid drips SLOWLY off the back of a spoon.

9. Leave the syrup to one side to cool and proceed with cooking the dough.

10. To stop the dough from sticking to your spoon as you scoop it from the bowl place your teaspoon in warm water prior to making your dough ball.

11. Using a deep fat fryer or pan full of hot oil place small scoops of the dough mixture and fry until a light yellow colour then remove from the oil to drain.

12. Once all the dough has been used (or required number of balls have been made), refry the loukoumades until a rich golden colour and place in a bowl.

13. Pour over the cooled syrup and just prior to serving, sprinkle with cinnamon powder and sesame seeds.

GALAKTOBOUREKO – Custard Pie

This wonderfully sweet and delicious dessert is made with philo pastry and homemade custard and is a great sweet to eat with a little tsikoudia!

INGREDIENTS

350g Sugar
1.5 Litres Milk
1 Egg Yolk
2 Egg Whites
130g Butter
Philo Pastry Sheets
Vanilla Essence
3 Heaped Dessert Spoons Corn Flour
3 Level Dessert Spoons Semolina
375 ml Water
¼ of a Lemon

PREPARATION

1. To make the syrup - Mix the sugar, water, the juice from the lemon and a few drops of vanilla essence in a pan and place on a low heat to bring slowly to a simmer. Whilst this is warming go to Step 2.

2. Melt some butter and brush around a large square oven dish before layering up to seven individual sheets of philo pastry into the pan. Each sheet should be brushed with melted butter before placing into the pan and the edges should be draped over the sides to allow folding in later.

3. To make the custard – Whisk the egg yolk and 2 egg whites with 500ml of milk and a few drops of vanilla essence in a pan on a medium heat.

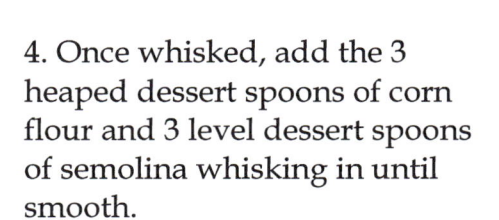

4. Once whisked, add the 3 heaped dessert spoons of corn flour and 3 level dessert spoons of semolina whisking in until smooth.

5. Pour the custard mixture over the philo pastry.

Cooking With Katerina

6. Fold the pastry edges over on top of the custard.

7. Add 6 more layers of philo pastry, brushing with butter each time and ensure the final layer is well coated with the melted butter.

8. Once completed, cut through the pie with a sharp knife to create portion sized triangle shapes.

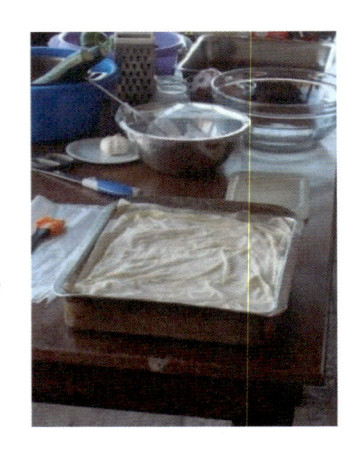

9. Sprinkle the top lightly with water and bake in an oven at 180 C for 45 minutes.

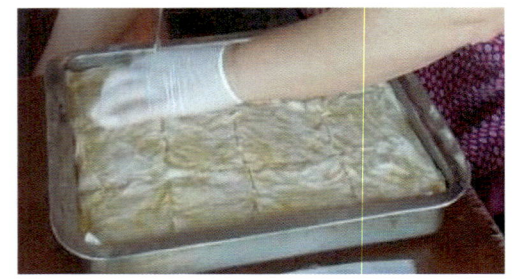

10. When you place the galaktoboureko in the oven, remove the heat from your syrup and allow it to cool.

11. After removing your galaktoboureko allow it to cool for 5 minutes before slowly pouring your syrup mix over the top.

12. Cool in a fridge before serving to ensure custard has set.

KALITSOUNIA – Cheese Pies (With Honey)

A savoury delight with a sweet twist. They are real favourites of the North-West region of Crete known as Sfakia.

Experiment with different shapes of pastry to find one that you like best and remember to use the sweetest honey you can find. The Cretan honey that is made from the pollen of the wild thyme plants is especially good with these wonderful pies.

INGREDIENTS

FOR THE PASTRY

500ml Water
2 Tablespoons of Yeast
50ml Raki (Tsikoudia)
1 kg All Purpose Flour
2 Teaspoons of Salt

FOR THE FILLING

1 kg Myzithra Cheese
1 kg Malaka Cheese (grated)
2 Teaspoons of Salt
½ Cup of Mint Leaves
1 Dessert Spoon of Corn Flour

1 Egg (To add shine to the pastry)
Honey

PREPARATION

1. Dissolve the yeast in the warm water; add the 50ml raki and 2 teaspoons of salt.

2. Gradually add the flour, mixing it in with your hands until you have a firm and elastic dough.

3. Place your pastry in a plastic bag and leave in a warm place for at least 30 minutes.

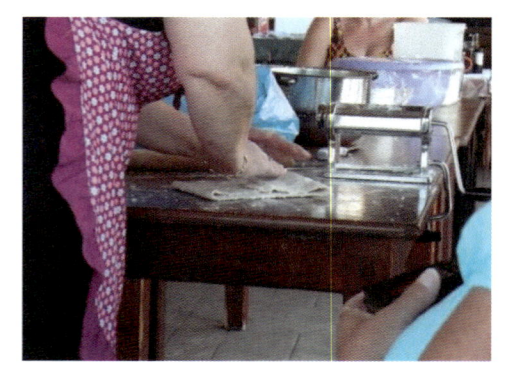

4. Once your pastry has rested, roll it out to lengths of approximately 30cm and ½ cm thick. Place these lengths on top of each other and place back into the plastic bag for another 20 minutes.

5. Whilst the pastry is resting it is now time to make the cheese pie filling.

6. Add the Myzithra, Malaka, corn flour, salt and mint to a large mixing bowl.

7. Mix the ingredients by a combination of squeezing and stirring them together with your hand.

8. Once fully mixed together continue with your pastry.

9. The pastry should now have formed into a layered block. Using a pastry roller (pasta machine) on setting '0' roll and fold cut portions of the pastry until it is approximately 30cm in length.

10. Change the setting to '3' and place the pastry through the machine again.

11. To make an even finer pastry, run it one last time through your machine on setting '6'.

TO MAKE OVEN BAKED CHEESE PIES

12. Cut the pastry sheets into hand width sized squares.

13. Take a small ball of cheese mix and place in the centre of the pastry square.

14. Fold over the corners and press down the edges to seal the pastry square.

15. Place on grease proof paper in a flat oven dish and brush with a beaten egg.

16. Sprinkle with sesame seeds and bake in an oven at 180 C for 15-20 minutes until golden brown.

17. Serve either hot or cold as a delicious savoury treat..

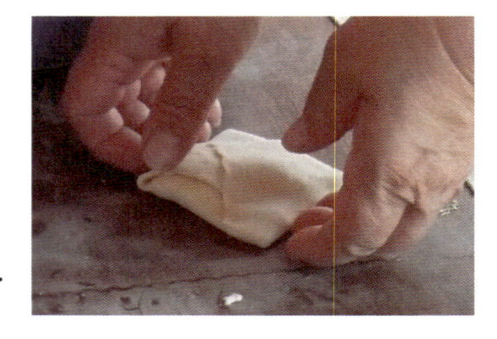

TO MAKE FRIED CHEESE PIES WITH HONEY

18. Place a saucer on your pastry strip and cut around the edge with a sharp knife to make a pastry circle.

19. Place a ball of the cheese mixture into the centre of your pastry circle.

20. Fold over to create a semi-circle and crimp the edges to make a sealed pocket.

21. Fry in hot oil until crisp.

22. Just before serving, drizzle honey over the top of your cheese pie.

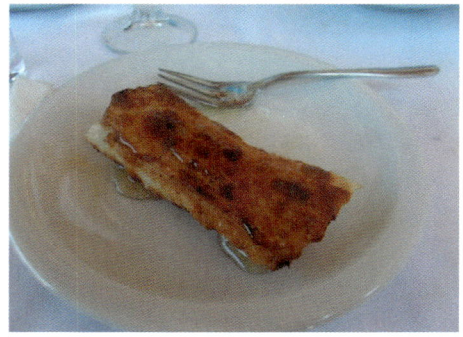

BAKLAVA – Sweet flaky pastry with nuts

Sweet bites of pastry that are jam-packed with nuts and syrup that will have any sweet-tooth grinning with pleasure. Home-made baklava is a fantastic end to any Cretan meal.

INGREDIENTS- For approximately 15-20 portions

Filling
1 Packet Philo Pastry Sheets
120g Pistachio Nuts
180g Walnuts
125g Almonds
500g Butter
½ Teaspoon Cloves
1 teaspoon Cinnamon
2 Dessert Spoons Sugar

Syrup
500ml Water 750g Sugar
Vanilla Sugar Sachet
Juice of ½ Lemon

PREPARATION

1. Coarsely crush the nuts adding the cloves, cinnamon and 2 dessert spoons of sugar and mix together.

2. Melt 500g of butter and use it to liberally brush the bottom of a large square oven pan.

3. Lay 2 sheets of philo pastry in your pan, brushing between and over them with the butter. It doesn't matter if your sheets drape over the side of your pan as they can be folded in later.

4. Sprinkle a handful of your nut mixture in an even layer over the pastry.

5. Fold in your pastry sides and brush with butter before laying another sheet of the pastry on top which you brush with butter before sprinkling more of your nut mixture over.

6. Repeat until the dish is full or you have used up your nut mixture, remembering to brush each sheet with butter.

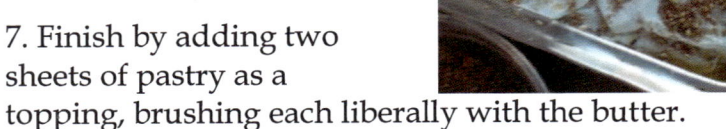

7. Finish by adding two sheets of pastry as a topping, brushing each liberally with the butter.

8. Sprinkle with water to keep the pastry moist whilst cooking in the oven.

9. Before placing in the oven, cut through the uncooked baklava into the shape and size portions you wish to serve.

10. Make your syrup by adding 500ml water, 750g of sugar the juice of half a lemon and a 9g vanilla sugar sachet into a saucepan and bringing to the boil for 5 minutes, stirring occasionally. Leave it to one side to cool as the baklava cooks.

11. Place the baklava in a hot oven at 180 C for 40 minutes to 1 hour until the baklava is a rich, golden brown.

12. Pour your cooled syrup over the baklava and allow it to seep into the pastry and filling before serving.

KRASOKOULORA – Cookies made with wine

Deliciously crunchy cookies with sesame seed and a hint of cinnamon that are made without any eggs. The best thing about these Krasokoulora are that they can keep for up to 3 months…if you can leave them alone that is.

INGREDIENTS – enough for 200-300 cookies

200g Sesame Seeds
500g Sugar
750ml Olive Oil
500ml White Wine
1 Table Spoon Cinnamon (Ground)
1 Dessert Spoon Cloves (Ground)
2Kg Plain flour
1 Dessert Spoon Baking Soda
2 Dessert Spoons Baking Powder

Cooking With Katerina

PREPARATION

1. Put all the ingredients EXCEPT the flour into a large bowl and stir gently.

2. Slowly fold in the flour, mixing well with your hands until a firm dough is made.

3. Cover with cling film and leave for 10-15 minutes.

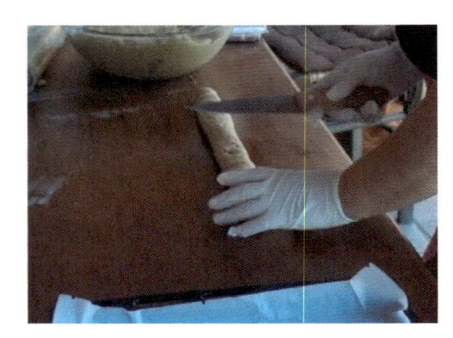

4. Line a baking tray with greaseproof paper.

5. Take a handful of dough and roll it out into a long roll approximately 2cm thick.

6. Cut into smaller sections and shape into whichever cookie shape you desire and place on the baking tray. You can sprinkle and roll the dough with more sesame seeds at this point.

7. Bake at 180 C for 25 minutes.

8. Allow to cool before serving, they are great with a little raki.

SFOUNGARI LEMONI - Lemon Sponge

Sweet, tart and bursting with lemon freshness, this lemon sponge is a treat that you will want to share.

INGREDIENTS

<u>For The Sponge</u>
6 Eggs
Zest and Juice of 1 Lemon
1Kg Sugar
1Kg Plain Flour
Sunflower Oil
2 Dessert Spoons Baking Powder

<u>For The Syrup</u>
750ml Water
250g Sugar

Zest and Juice of 2 Lemons

For The Cream
1 Litre Water
Zest and Juice of 2 Lemons
400g Sugar
1 Egg Yolk
Sachet (15g) of Vanilla Sugar
4 Dessert Spoons Corn Flour

PREPARATION

1. Start by making the sponge; Add the eggs, lemon zest, lemon juice, 2 dessert spoons of baking powder and 1Kg of sugar into a large mixing bowl.

2. Whisk the ingredients of the bowl as you slowly add the 1Kg of plain flour to make your sponge mixture.

3. Using sunflower oil, grease the bottom and sides of your cake tin and then sprinkle with a little flour.

4. Pour the sponge mixture into the cake tin.

5. Bake in a pre-heated oven at 175 C for 45 minutes to 1 hour. Check the cake is cooked by placing a knife into the center of the sponge, when cooked it should come out clean.

6. Whilst the sponge is cooking prepare the syrup by mixing all the syrup ingredients together in a large saucepan on a medium heat. Stir to mix the contents together then leave to boil for 5 minutes before removing from the heat to cool.

 To make the cream filling and topping

7. In a large jug or bowl add 1 litre of water, 125ml lemon juice, the zest of 2 lemons and a sachet of vanilla sugar.

8. Mix the contents together, then remove a quarter of the liquid and keep to one side.

9. Put the remaining liquid in a pan and bring to the boil.

10. Using the quarter of the liquid removed in Step 8, mix in 4 dessert spoons of corn flour ensuring there are no lumps in the mixture.

11. Once your pan is boiling, slowly whisk in the corn flour mix to make the cream. Keep the pan on the heat as you whisk it in.

12. Once it has turned to a thick cream take it off the heat and whisk in 1 egg yolk and 400g of sugar.

13. Leave the cream to thicken and cool.

14. Once your sponge has cooked, allow it to cool slightly before cutting through the centre of the sponge to leave a top and a bottom half.

15. Drizzle half of your syrup over the bottom part of your sponge, then thickly spread your cream across the bottom half.

16. Turn the top half upside down and place on top of your cream layered bottom half so that the cut side is facing upwards.

17. Drizzle with the remaining syrup and spread the remaining cream over the top and sides of your sponge. Smooth the cream with a metal spatula or knife.

18. Sprinkle with flaked almonds if required, and place in a fridge to cool and set.

19. Serve chilled with ice cream or cream.

ROSAKIA – Mini Chocolate Swirl Cakes

A chocolate centre surrounded by sweet, juicy pastry will make you want to try 'just one more' of these mini cakes. You may see these little sweet dessert cakes at weddings and other celebrations where they are warmly received for their subtle sweetness and chocolate flavour.

INGREDIENTS

2cm Cube of Fresh Yeast
500ml Sunflower Oil
500ml Milk
500g Flour
2g Vanilla Powder
Cocoa Powder

For The Syrup
1Kg Sugar
750ml Water
Lemon Zest from ½ a Lemon

PREPARATION

1. Dissolve the yeast in a cup of warm water to which has been added a teaspoon of sugar. Leave to one side to rest.

2. Make the syrup by adding the sugar, water and lemon zest to a saucepan and bringing to a boil for 10 minutes. Once the time is up, leave to one side to cool. This will be used after baking the rosakia.

3. The yeast should now have started to create air bubbles. Place it in a mixing bowl along with the sunflower oil, milk and vanilla powder. Add flour slowly as you use a food mixer to create soft pastry dough that is not too dry.

4. Take a handful of the pastry mix and place it in a separate bowl along with two dessert spoons of cocoa powder. Mix until well blended and a rich brown colour throughout.

5. Cover and leave both dough mixtures to rest in a warm place for 5-10 minutes.

6. Using the plain dough, roll out to a length that is approximately 1 inch (2.5 cm) thick and then chop this into pieces that are around double its thickness.

7. Roll out the cocoa dough in the same way but make the pieces half the size of your plain dough.

8. Thinly roll out the plain dough into a thin cigar shape length and add a balled up piece of cocoa dough to one end. Wrap the chocolate ball with the plain dough and place on a baking tray lined with greaseproof paper.

Ensure there is a gap between your cakes as they will expand slightly as they cook.

9. Leave to rest for 15 minutes before placing in a preheated oven at 200 C for 25 minutes or until they the pastry turns golden brown.

10. Whilst still hot, place in the bowl of syrup and stir gently to avoid breaking the cakes.

11. Drain in a colander and allow to cool before serving.

Cooking With Katerina

Printed in Great Britain
by Amazon